AF333099

Ten Year Reunion

Poetry of Then and Now

James P. Wagner (Ishwa)

Ten Year Reunion

Copyright © 2016 by James P. Wagner (Ishwa)

Published by Local Gems Press

www.localgemspoetrypress.com

All rights reserved. No part of this book may be
reproduced or transmitted in any form or by any means
without written permission of the author.

*For the class of 2004
and everyone else who ever felt
"stuck in between"
two entirely different worlds*

Introduction by the Author

As one who can do basic math might expect—2014 was the 10 year reunion for the graduating high school class of 2004. When we were in school we always imagined that reunions were something the school itself planned—but obviously, as the reunion got to be closer and closer we realized that wasn't the case. Somehow, and I'm still not exactly sure how, with the president of our class out in California, I ended up being the one to attempt to organize something. Like any event with a lot of people, mishaps ensued, and we finally decided on an informal gathering at one of our favorite local Northport bars, Napper Tandy's.

Although I was fortunate to maintain close friendships with a few people from high school, many of these faces I hadn't seen in years—some not since graduation. I had no idea what most of them were up to, or what they had spent the last decade doing, but yet there was a serene type of familiarity being surrounded by these people again—these people who I had spent so many of my formative years with—even if it was just for a little while. It got me thinking—

thinking hard, perhaps even over-thinking (as many people who know me can attest that I do sometimes) about life, adulthood, security, nostalgia and a whole lot more. It got me thinking about how different the world is from the time we were in high school until now.

It got me thinking about how much the world has changed since 911—the impact on security, laws, permissions, and how the world is far more uptight now than it was back then. It got me thinking about Generation Y, or Millennials and how many of us yearn for a time long gone, or at the very least, have a longing to belong to something again—to be part of a community while many of us report feeling completely isolated despite our 24-hour connection to the internet.

So I did what all poets do when their minds start racing—I started writing. Some of it came quick, some of it took forever, but here is what I got. After many Zen-like meditation sessions with the goal of remembering the past in as close to perfect detail as I could remember, I have to say that I am now convinced more than ever that the generation I grew up in—the mid-80s children, are a breed like no other— growing up in a very narrow transition period between the ages of analog and digital. We are old enough to remember a time when going outside to play was still a thing, before we had the internet in our pocket—and yet we were young enough when computers started to take over that we adapted to them quickly. I wonder if this is the reason why many of us feel a nostalgia that might be just a shade thicker than other generations— in the sense that when our childhood ended literally an entire era ended and a new one began.

In some ways the generation born now is a generation I can never completely connect with—we might speak the same digital language, but they never existed in a time before that language was predominant. They never remember the things that myself, and the fellow members of the class of 2004 and the surrounding years can remember. They don't remember the anguish of CD players in their pockets— they don't remember having to choose between the internet or the telephone on a dial-up line, they don't remember how the 90s was an age when the world seemed to be on a mission to make it fun to be a kid— and they don't remember the days when we weren't connected to everyone else around the entire planet, but somehow barely connected to the people right next to us.

These poems are poems from the point of view of a member of this very narrow sub-generation. It is poetry of then and now, submitted for the world and generations to come (should it reach that far) to read and hopefully understand us a little better.

Thanks for reading.

~ James P. Wagner (Ishwa)

Foreword

It's amazing "what a difference a decade makes." These lines from the eponymous poem of James P. Wagner's "Ten Year Reunion" sum up the sentiment of the entire book. *Ten Year Reunion* is brimming with nostalgia for a time when the Internet existed, but did not monopolize our lives.

I have read that Millennials, especially those of us born in the 80s, are excessively nostalgic. We've been accused of clinging to our childhoods and the cultural artifacts that defined them. Enabled by technology, we buy DVDs of our favorite shows, play old video games on emulators, and reminisce with each other via memes and social media posts. Every generation seems to long for its "good old days," but many Millenials constantly seek to re-experience the joys of their formative years.

Those of us born in the 80s were raised during a time like no other. We were the "video generation": children raised in a time when home video, audio recording, and personal computers were ubiquitous. We were raised with unparalleled access to entertainment via VHS tapes, audio tapes and CDs, video game consoles, computer games and learning programs (which became increasingly deep and complex with the advent of the CD ROM), and an increasingly diverse offering of television networks, some of which were specifically tailored for kids. Not all of us had access to all of these technological marvels, but many of us had access to at least one. While they may not have been the center of our lives, many of our fondest memories are at least loosely associated with some form of media.

As the 90s drew to a close, another technological marvel was becoming more and more commonplace: the Internet. The Internet of the 90s would be almost unrecognizable by today's standards. It wasn't essential or something one was always connected to. It was ugly, it was slow, and it was widely considered a luxury. The Internet grew up with Millennials. We got to see it evolve and evolve with it. We (fortunately) lived through most of our formative years before Web 2.0 and the advent of "social" media.

Those of us born in the 80s spent most of our childhood without the Internet, but were still children when we were introduced to it. We can remember a time when, as countless memes announce, social networking meant picking up the (home) phone and calling a friend or walking down the street to a friend's house to play *in person*. However, we also get the Internet and its culture. We understand it the way only those who have grown up with it could. For better or worse, we helped make online culture what it is today.

Many Millennials, especially those of us in close-knit suburbia, grew up in a time of relative prosperity and abundance, and thus were largely unaware of the world outside of our bubbles. This, compounded by our experience with the Internet, and its absence during our childhoods, leaves many with the sense that they grew up in safer or simpler times. This accounts for a large dose of Millennial nostalgia, especially when one considers the event that served as a wake-up call for many of us.

Some of us were in high school on September 11, 2001. A few us were fresh out of high school, and some were still in middle school. No matter how far along we were in our academic careers, we were young, and we were impacted. For many of us, it was an abrupt end, or the beginning of the end of our childhoods. Perhaps another reason many Millennials seem extra nostalgic is because we vividly remember a time before 9/11 and can see the stark contrast between our world now and our world then.

Regardless of the reasons, *Ten Year Reunion* is filled with moments of nostalgia for a time when technology was rapidly evolving, free AOL CDs made the best frisbees, research was done on paper, and cell phones were a privilege and a luxury. Its poems are also deeply personal. James bares a part of himself for the readers to see. Even I learned a thing or two, and I knew him back then.

~ Nick Hale

Publisher for Local Gems Press, Best-Selling Editor, Author of *Broken Reflections*

Table of Contents

Ten Year Reunion

The ten year high school reunion
Something they made movies about
Episodes about on sitcoms
Something that seemed
So far off
So far away
Our ten year reunion
It didn't seem real
But here it was
2014
Ten years for the class of 2004
What a difference
A decade makes

Nothing planned by the school itself
It was up to our class
To organize it
What a nightmare…
Several failed attempts later
We gather at Napper Tandy's
A Northport favorite bar
Informally
Seemed fitting for the budget many of us had…

Some of us in graduate school
Or recently out of law school
Most still not entirely settled in our careers
Something none of us
Would have expected
When looking from high school onward
Yet here we were
The people that many of us
Had spent our formative years with
Many we knew longer
Than just the four years of high school
Some all the way back to middle school
Elementary school
Pre-school
The faces we saw every day
The faces we grew up with
Whether we were friends or not
The familiarity
Was comforting
A snapshot back
To our roots
To the time when we were all
Figuring out who we were
What we were
What we were going to be
Some of us, still figuring that out

Ten Year Reunion

Others having known it for a long time.

Sharing tales of the past decade
Over drinks
And food.
What colleges we went to
What jobs we had now
What businesses we ran
how many kids, some of us had
the hierarchies of high school
the sub-categories we used to fit into
who we used to hang around with
the clubs we were in
the sub-cultures and classifications we all had
not really relevant anymore.

The feeling of being around these people again
has a sobering effect
a clarity
that ten years
had come and gone
the path behind me is farther
than it seems
everything my mother and father
aunt and uncle
grandmother and grandfather always said

about time being a flash
that I used to ignore
was true
as I walked around there
talking and sharing stories
I remembered the time
When despite our differences
all of us had so much,
a daily routine,
a school
this town in common.
And however much we may have scattered like the
wind
in a world where many of us feel uprooted
un-centered, imbalanced
when this last decade meant
an entire generation of change
one thing that would always be true
is the people around me on this night
the ten year reunion
would always,
always
be the class
of 2004.

First Day of High School

After 7 years in a newly opened
Catholic school
And 1 year at East Northport middle
My first thought
On my first day of high school
Was how huge the place was
I'd been there before,
My aunt had a job teaching English there
for awhile
So I'd seen the small commons
With all the lockers
But the gym
The labs
The theater
Were all new to me
"How am I supposed to get to my classes in
4 minutes?" I thought
And sometimes that proved harder than one
would think
A glimpse at the commons
Right in the center of the school
With the four "wells" for members of each grade

To hang out in
Hundreds of other students
Most of whom already knew
Where to go
How to get there
Who to hang out with
While I was still figuring it all out
"Where's the L wing?"
"Which one is the cafeteria?"
"Which way is the library?"
"For the love of God…could someone have mercy
and help me find my locker?!"
Just a few of the dozens of questions I remember
Asking that day.
But even then
When reunions seemed like a far off
Fantasy future
I remember feeling that those 4 years
Were going to be big
More than 14 later
I would look back and say
They weren't big…
They were huge.

My First Cell Phone

I got my first cell phone
When I was 13
Well…it wasn't really mine
My mom bought it
For me to use.
It was crappy little phone
Not a flip phone
Pre-flip, pre-paid,
With a 20-minute
Phone card.
I got it when I was going
On the 8th Grade Boston trip –
We still had it back then
Before 9-11 got it cancelled
For a few years at least.
It was in my backpack, never on
Heck,
I didn't even know its number
And didn't need to
Because it was never meant to receive calls
But make them in case
Of emergency

And after the trip
I kept it, just in case.
It sat inside my backpack
Except when I took it out
to show my friends
Who were all jealous of me
Couldn't believe I had a cell phone!

I got my first real cell phone when I was 16
One with an actual plan
100 minutes a month
And if I went over those 100 minutes,
I had to pay for it myself.
Made many calls free after 9pm, to make sure
I never had to pay that overage.

Last week when I stepped out
For a late lunch at 3 o'clock
At Mario's Pizza,
The same one I'd been going to
Since first grade
When I was in catholic school
5 kids from my old school
6th graders by the looks of them if I remember
The uniforms correctly
All of them sitting around a table near me

And while I was eating and flipping through
One of my biographies of Benjamin Franklin
All of them
Were checking their recent test grades
On their smartphones.

The Playground

When I was 7
it was huge.
I enjoyed my Nintendo
I loved television
but the playground
was my favorite place to go
after school
to see the friends I made there
who met up with me 3 or 4 times a week.

After school
weekends
vacations
I'd get my mother
grandmother, grandfather
to take me there
to climb the hill
to rock on the swings
to slide down the slide
and run back up it.

Ten Year Reunion

My friends and I played
all sorts of games
I was often King
or Prince of the castle
while they ran to slay the dragons
or to sneak into the no boy's allowed
section the girls had made
and they'd scream and run away
and it would all be ours!

Even today, the playground is there
a bit different now.
More plastic
a bit more safety conscious
still maintained and funded
by the town.

I drive past there every so often
and every time I do
and see the swings blowing
back and forth
in the wind
the empty tunnels
the vacant slides
I feel sorry for the children
who are children now

and lament
all the adventures
they are missing out on.

The Library

It was my sanctuary
During my freshman year when I had
Only 2 friends
Grandfathered in from 8th grade
My first year of public school
Neither of them had the same lunch period
As I did
So each day,
After a quick trip to the cafeteria where I sat with
Tao and Wilson
Foreign students from China and Honduras
Who also had no one else to sit with
I took my bag and ran to the library
Where mountains of books
And the internet were waiting.

I scoured all ends of that library,
From the poetry books
To the Star Wars expanded universe directories
All under the watchful eye
Of Mr. Hanley the librarian
Who always greeted me with a smile

and a handshake.
The internet was still fairly new
To us all at that time
I'd spend lunch hours checking emails
That I wasn't getting
From imaginary people
Scanning fanfiction.net
Looking up the website for Toonami to check
The upcoming anime schedules.
I had many good times in that library
And as I made more friends,
I had many good times
Outside of that library
As well.

15 Songs

In 2001
My sophomore year of high school
I got the new Gorillaz CD
They were a cool band
With cool songs
And this CD had 15 of them.
So thankful we had come so far from the days of
Records
8-Track tapes
Cassettes
My CD player
Came everywhere with me
Going through the anguish
Of trying to fit the big round device
Into regular-sized pockets
I would listen to my songs
While walking in the hallway between classrooms
I had my favorites on the CD
But listened to all of them
Got to know all of them
Just me and the band's music.
Little did I know

That by the time of my 10 year high school reunion
The devices we'd have would be 15 times smaller
Hold over 15,000 songs on them
And that it wouldn't be very often
That anyone would listen
To an entire album
Anymore.

911 As A Sophomore

It started out like any other day
Second week of my second year
Of high school
Second period
Math class
Going through the anguish
Of trying to concentrate
When still half asleep
Not yet used to the early days again
After summer
The announcement came in the last 5 minutes
of class
"Boys and girls, we have just received word
That there has been a terrible accident at the World
Trade Center."
An accident
I remember that wording specifically
None of us really knew what to make of that
A moment later the bell rang
And I got up to go to third period business class
Taught by Mr. Campbell
The most laid back

Hilarious teacher
Only a few year away from retirement
And as a veteran of the Vietnam War
Not one to take the silly dramas and trials
Of dealing with teenagers too seriously.
Upon entering the classroom
The television
One of the few active,
Non VCR/DVD player-only televisions
That happened to be in the classroom
Where we normally had class
By pure happenstance
Was on
Turned to the news.
We didn't do any classwork that period
Watched the footage
Of the first plane
Followed by the second plane
Saw one of the towers collapse live
Saw a replay of the other one
The smoke growing and growing
We were all very confused
No motive or reason had yet been released
The casualty numbers were climbing
Two classmates from that period excused
Sent to the office

Where they could make phone calls
To try to find out information
About their parents who worked
In the city.
And Mr. Campbell
Standing there, arms crossed
Shaking his head
With a somber
Sullen
Saddened look
That I never saw on him before
Or since
"You don't know it know," he said,
"but this is going to be the day that will define
your entire generation."
More than a decade later
I can only say
How right he was.

Corporal Chris

I met you in 8th grade history class
You had a cast on your arm
For the few first months
From some sports-related injury
Or activity you took part in over the summer
We didn't talk all that much
I was the new kid and you
Already had a lot of friends
We never really knew each other
all that well
But I do remember
Your patriotism
After 911
Claiming that we all needed to stick together
In this hard time
Weren't a fan of the protests in the commons
Claiming that America deserved the attacks
Joined the counter-protest
Beaming with pride
For your country.
You were one of the many people from
Our graduating class

Ten Year Reunion

Who joined the military
The Marines for you
The first ones
By land by air by sea
It seemed fitting
With how you always were
I heard about your death
In the line of duty
Not long after it happened
A town hero
Who we now remember each year
With the run in the East Northport grid

I think of you, and how young you were when
you died
Standing up for what you believed in
Fighting for the country you loved
And remember that 911 was right here
And it really did
Define
Our entire generation

Just Hanging Out

"Wanna hang out?"
"When?"
"Friday Night?"
"What time?"
"8?"
"What do you wanna do?"
"Food?"
"Where?"
"Apps?"
"Sure."
In making these plans I remember a time
When friends would converge
Randomly
Unplagued by classes
When work was a part-time thing
Meant to give you pocket money
To make your own adventures
And hanging out
Was not preempted
By a shopping list of specifics
When people weren't so rigid
With their likes and dislikes

Their dos and don'ts
When we still had space
And time
To find out new things about ourselves
Let the chips fall where they may
And the company you kept
Was the only constant
That you needed.

The B Minus

She couldn't stop staring at it
staring
staring
disbelief
anguish
wondering if she was really awake
or still dreaming
she knew from science class
that a lack of R.E.M. sleep over prolonged periods
would result in impaired higher cognitive function
and she knew she'd been burning the candle
at both ends
for quite some time
day time and night time blending together
but this
this must be a dream.

She'd gotten straight A's since there were A's to
be had
just like they expected of her
just like they've told her
since she could remember

the grades that would determine her future
her college
her salary
what her future would be like
this was NOT a game
she could NOT mess this up

She'd worked so hard
so much she could do
so much she was capable of

Interact club
chess club
school play
mathletes
volleyball team
environmental team
science ambassador
pre-law society

There are only so many hours in a day
no time to goof off
no time to waste
she shouldn't have wasted
those 3 hours for dinner and the movies
2 weeks back for her birthday

her father told her it was a bad idea
too many distractions
but she hadn't seen her friends in so long
outside of school
and she wanted to indulge
but it was obviously a bad idea
because she could have been studying
could have been studying
and maybe
even in this sleep deprived state
she would have known it all instinctually –
was this the end of it all?
Her 105 average
Valedictorian
full scholarship to Harvard
career as a doctor
researcher
all the opportunities her parents never had –
would she disappoint them?

holding it back
holding it back
grabbed both sides of the paper
yanked at it from both ends
fell to her knees
and cried.

The Diskette

I used to love diskettes
Diskettes
The 1.44 megabyte capacity
Memory disk that was newer than the
old huge floppy disks we had in computer class
in 1993
they were a jump forward
used regularly with the new computers
we all started getting in the later 90s
household computers
with access to the internet
and in 2002-2004
I put everything on diskettes.
Went to my local store which stocked them
in many different colors
a green one for this story
a red one for my poems
a blue one for my novel
I'd password protect them
give them out to my friends
store them in my plastic safe
hide them in the wall

pretend like one of them was a secret decoder disk
used to break into high security places
they made me feel so advanced
like out of beast wars
or transformers
or some amazing television show.
But today,
even though I can hold in the palm of my hand
or on my keychain
a flash drive
capable of holding 25,000 times
that amount of memory
and even though my laptop doesn't even have
a disk drive anymore
and even if it did
1.44 megabytes would barely hold
a single picture
none of the new technology we have had
since then
has made me feel as cool
as those 4.5 inch floppies.

The Hill

Out at the edge of the property
Of my high school
Across the circular driveway for busses to pull up
Past the parking lot
Was a staircase on the hill
The hill
We called it.
Where all the kids who smoked
Would line up after school
Ritualistically
Take out their cigarettes
And light up
Sometimes a shady shopkeeper from downtown
Would drive up to the hill
To discreetly sell cigarettes to
Those who couldn't legally smoke
Or to those who could smoke with the intent
Of them spreading them around.
I always thought the hill was where the
Wannabes and the posers gathered
And yet, at the ten year reunion
I could see if nothing else

Some friendships that formed there
Chatting after school
Still held strong.
Now that New York
The nanny state
Raised the smoking age
From 18 to 21
And no high school kid
Can legally smoke
I wonder if people still gather at the hill
after school.

Buying A Video Game

We grew up on them
Video games
Once upon a time seen as
"just a thing that kids do."
Many of us nearing or past our 30s
Still spending countless hours
Playing them.
Video games came before we did
But we were the first generation
To be born into a world
With Nintendo
Super Nintendo
Sega Genesis
Atari
Original handheld Gameboys.
I remember when Super Mario and Duckhunt
Were new
I remember the first Sonic the Hedgehog game
I remember when Pokemon Red and Blue were
New and we got to use the link cable to trade
Smash Bros. for the N64
Remember seeing advertisements in magazines

For Dreamcast
Gamecube
Playstation 2
Xbox…the first one
Not Xbox One which I never really
Figured out why they named them backwards.
Our lunch periods in high school would consist
of conversations
About various games we were playing
After school hangouts
Consisting of game tournaments
And smash sessions
The occasional trip to an arcade
Back when the local Nathan's
Had one
Before it became that sushi place that failed
within a year
But as more systems have come out since then
And online gaming took over
Where people play with others people hundreds
of miles away
When the arcade scene has dried up
And in the downloadable world
Where they are always trying to sell you extras
Selling you bits and pieces of games at a time
I miss the days when video games

Had a live
In-person
Social element to them
When they would bring people together
And of course
I miss being able to pay one price
And buy an entire game
Simple, easy, honorable
Without DRM.

Chess Club

What a bunch of characters
We had in our chess club
Future lawyers
Mathletes
Foreign students who seemed bored
With most of the other clubs
Some bad players
Some good
Some really good
Mr. Ritz
A Spanish teacher
Heading up our eclectic group of
Sort-of misfits
Constantly telling us we were there because
"we had no friends"
With that cheeky smirk of his
A great instructor
Playing him made me a much stronger player
Unlike the teacher at the previous chess club
I had been a part of
Ritz was not afraid to destroy us
And tear our games apart

Ten Year Reunion

His honesty
Made us want to improve
And it showed by the fact that we took in more
Trophies each year
Than the football team did
In my entire 4 years of high school
I was first board in my senior year
Probably thanks to my constant lunch-time games
In the Spanish resource room with Mr. Ritz
It was a title I was proud of
Despite the fact that
 we didn't get a pep rally
Or cheerleaders
Or even a bus half the time
To go to the other schools
To face the other school's teams
And the fact that probably more than half
the school didn't even know
We had a chess team
It was a fun safe haven for all of us
Wednesday afternoons after school
And even though I still play chess online
Still play in a league with the retired guys
Down at my library
Still meet up with some of my chess club buddies
And occasionally still even see Mr. Ritz for a game

Here or there
There was nothing like my high school chess club
Or the games that we played
While we had it.

Powdered Wigs

It was some of the most fun I had
In my four years in high school
Each season
When Powdered Wigs
The school's theater troupe
Would put on our annual musical.
Fiddler on the Roof,
How to Succeed in Business (without really trying)
Kiss me Kate
And *Annie Get Your Gun*
Were the four chosen for my four years.
We were the schools entertainers
We were the ones
Unafraid to perform
The school play always
Being a huge deal each year
Often 40-60 of us
In the cast
Huge ensemble
A creative team, getting to meet
And make friends with people
From different grades

The people in the grade above me especially
Were riots
Hilarious, colorful people
Some of them would later make it
To Broadway.
The theater itself was huge
Big balcony
Built in orchestra pit
That the school orchestra would use
To play the score for our play.
My own theater teacher would accumulate
A huge crew to work on the sets
And the props
And the lighting.
I still act today,
Am still in plays today
And I have to tell you that
I've been in theaters that have been less impressive
Than the one at my high school
That's how good it was.
I will never forget those long days after school
Never forget the months of practice
The jokes, the laughs, the goofs, the improv
Never forget the hard work we all put in for it
When now, in my adulthood, 15 extra minutes
Practically anywhere, seems like a burden.

And in my adulthood
In a world where people are divided and scattered
I will never forget the camaraderie,
The working together towards a goal,
The ambition and the fun
Of Powdered Wigs.

The Small Commons

By the time of my junior year
After my various awkward phases
When I had managed to amass a rather large
Assortment
Of friends from various categories
Of high school
There were certain rituals we had formed
Hangouts,
Meetups,
Activities, etc
But every day
In the early morning
Before first period
When the busses had dropped people off
And I walked in
We all met up in the space known
As the small commons
The huge circular hall of locker after locker
By the English wing at the east entrance of
The school
Facing Elwood Road.
Dozens of us

Ten Year Reunion

All unhappy with the early, early hour
That we were forced to be there
Using each other's company to cope with
The inconvenience
Discussing the previous nights episodes of the
Various shows we watched
Sharing video game strategies
Complaining about the various classes
Some of which we shared,
Some we didn't
Joking, laughing
Before the bell divided us
Sending is off to gym, or science
Or math or history or English
Or if we were lucky, a free period.
Though our days might have been divided,
We always had that morning
And as I've gone through life in various jobs
To running my own business
I sometimes long
For a small commons
Early morning ritual
With jokes and friends
To kick off my days with a smile.

High School Summer

Oh summer
how I miss you.
Not just because it's winter
and not just summer
but *summer*.

I remember high school summers,
the three-month vacation
that everyone
even the teachers
looked forward to.

Yes, it meant no more freezing weather,
shoveling
or frostbite.
And yes it meant that the trees would get
their leaves
and the weather would be warm.
But it was so much more than that.
It was SUMMER!
Beaches and ball games and hikes and bike rides
SUMMER!

No tests, or papers, no homework or studying.
FREEDOM!
Freedom from every day being taken up by
something we didn't want to do.
Freedom to do what you wanted to do,
with who you wanted to do it with.
For all of high school's popularity problems
most of us managed to amass a decent group
of friends
from the various sub-culture of sub-cultures.
Whether we were the jocks or the actors,
the chess club or the anime lovers,
the smokers, the drinkers, the druggies,
the mathletes, the pre-law society,
or an eclectic combination.
We managed to meet enough people
to do things with after-school.
And SUMMER
The convenience of geography and free time
made for many amazing adventures.

But now,
when the frost ends,
and the trees get their leaves,
thanks to years of college
where friendships came and went in a

four-year span
And geography is not convenient,
and free time for many means 2 weeks paid
vacation.
And full-time, double-full-time shifts are the
week to week.
When it takes 2 weeks to organize an outing
and 20-40 minutes to drive there.
In a world with more people than ever
and no social outlet
no common geography
to bind us all together,
Summer,
oh summer
you are just another season.

High School Guidance

College, college, college
SAT, Regents Exams
College
Grade improvement
College selections
College.
There were some other words in there
But every guidance session
Sounded the same.
"You need to prepare for college"
"You need to get your applications ready"
"You have to get all your ducks in a row…"
Pounding, pounding, pounding
Of the college mentality
Into our smallish brains.
Never presenting the option of trade school
Or vocational school
Using military school as a threatening "last resort"
Academic bully mentality
Of "If you don't get into college, you're a loser"
Never said, never stated outright
But looming over all of us, all the time.

State tests, grades,
Portfolios
A minimum of 6 applications
If you knew what was good for you
Because these 4 years of high school
Were basically worthless, right?
Just a qualifier for even more schooling
To go on and get degrees
In things that made no sense
No money
Because it's what we were *supposed* to do
Everyone ignoring the fact
That at the end of high school
After 12 years (at least)
Of schooling
We were being told flat out
The truth
That despite our looming quasi legal "adulthood"
That upon graduation
That we were qualified
Ultimately
To do nothing.

Visiting High School

When I was going there
From 2000-2004,
Visitors came back all the time
People who graduated the year before
2 years before
Or even 10 years before
People in their careers
Or just college students eager to visit
Their old friends
Or feeling nostalgia
For the heart of Northport
That was their home 5 days a week
For 4 years.
The doors, on all sides of the building
Were open
You technically were supposed to check in
With the front desk
But no one did
And no one cared.
Old friends who had come and gone
Would pop their heads into the classroom
Greeted warmly by the teachers

Hang out in the library
With Mr. Hanley,
The coolest librarian in the world
Free of the burden of classes and warning bells.

By the time I had graduated
I managed to get in 1 visit like this
1 stress-free, care-free visit
before the
post 9-11 hysteria
School shooting paranoia
Started keeping security guards at every door
Restrictions on visitor passes
And every entrance to the school locked.
I sometimes miss my high school
And want to go back there
And every time the thought crosses my mind
I sigh in disappointment
At the realization
I'd have a better chance
Of getting granted
A pass for visiting hours
At a prison.

A Simple Wish

In my later 20's I have come
To one inescapable conclusion
Everything I want
Costs money
They say that money can't buy you happiness
And maybe that's true
If you don't know what to show for
Focusing your financial means
On material possessions
Rather than experiences
That you will always remember
I find myself consistently seeking out new things
Never found a subject
Or an art
That didn't interest me
Balancing the budget
The price tags on
Tai Chi classes
Poetry readings
Art lessons
Music lessons
Spiritual retreats

I find myself shot backward in time
To a place
Where pretty much all of these things
Came packaged neatly
In a place I attended every day
For four years
Surrounded by people you knew
And called friends
I did a fair number of things in high school
Debate
Chess club
Acting
Business
Coffee houses
And more
But had I known then
What I know now
While weighing the contents of my wallet
Against the lessons
I want
I would have joined the marching band
Taken advantage of the many music lessons
That now cost so much
Would have tried out for a sports team
Now stuck in a world of e-sports where community
leagues are harder

And harder to find
Would have taken advantage
Of the foreign language classes
Maybe saved a little money
On all those Rosetta Stone programs
Would have
Would have
Would have
And as much as I don't believe
In regrets
Happy for who I am
Where I am now
Sometimes I can't help but wish
I had done just a little bit more
Taken a few more of those wonderful
Opportunities
While I had the chance

A Poem for Mike S.

We met in Camp Alvernia
The summer before 8th grade
I was 12, you were 14
The highest age group at the camp
When we got to go on the out-of-camp trips
To Adventureland
Laser Kingdom
Sports Plus (when it was still around.)
You were the cool kid at camp
Already working for your dad's construction
company
Extremely strong for your age
Never missed ringing the bell
At the strongman game
Could kayak faster than anyone
Loved to sail
Loved to swim
Always had money
Because of your job---gave out singles
And fives
To everyone who asked
When we were out on our trips

Ten Year Reunion

Everyone loved you
And you were always happy
On top of the universe—the entire world ahead
of you
I ran into you more than 12 years later at a
poetry reading
In Huntington
Cane in your hand
Limp in your walk from a motorcycle accident
You looked like life
Had beaten the heck out of you
Reading poems,
Sad poems with your head down
It took me awhile to recognize you
A shadow of yourself from in camp
We saw each other a few more times
Thanks to a mutual friend from the poetry world
And then you vanished again
Later that year I heard about your trip out to
Montauk
And the shotgun you put in your mouth
And I wondered what could have happened
Between the years
To change you so much
From the jovial life of camp
It makes me think

Of then and now
Of childhood and adulthood
About great expectations
And disappointments
About the lies our generation was told
And it makes me sad
That it's made you and many others
Think that the final option
Was your best option.

Confessions of Violence

There must be something wrong with me
I was one of those kids who had a toy-gun at age 5
Several actually
Used to watch all those late 80s, early 90s
cartoons with the lasers
And the explosions, transformers
Might morphing Power Rangers with
Big shiny weapons
And I had the replicas
There must be something wrong with me
I had the SuperSoaker 1500, 1600
1700, 2200 and that one with the backpack
water tank
That would shoot everyone
All the rapid fire nerf guns I'd use to bean
by friends
Repeatedly
Plastic imitations of the M-16 from Vietnam
That would make the
Bzzzzzzzztthththththt
From all the plastic marbles inside
I got a BB gun when I was 10

Didn't shoot my eye out, but shot hundreds of
coke cans
And other targets
There must be something wrong with me
My psychosis for violence went beyond that
Admittedly I was the kid who got into lots of
fights in school
But they started it
I took martial arts when I was 8
Fired real guns when I was 12
I had like 5000 Lego dudes
All with weapons
That I would bring to school
And have lego wars during math class
With my friend Ryan
And Mr. Leary
Most of the time
Was totally oblivious
Beyond that, I would constantly deface
My textbooks and workbooks
With the massive stick figure wars
That usually turned into mass stick figure genocide
Black and blue, sometimes red and purple
stick figures
Depending on what color pens I had
Shooting at each other from the opposite ends

of the page
Sometimes sneaking over to the other end's
fortress and planting
Big old crates of TNT that were labeled TNT
Underneath them
And boom, explosions of ink all over the pages
One of my teachers photocopies some of
those pages
Thinking I would go on a killing spree one day
And those stick figure wars would be the proof
Of my psychotic tendencies
And the fact that there was something wrong
with me
And yes in high school
I got ahold of the GTA games
Vice City
San Andreas
Rolling over people on the sidewalks
Driving by with my virtual Uzi and shooting
everyone
Killing the prostitutes I just banged to get my
money back
And firing those missile launches are the
police helicopters
That came to get me
I did all of these things

But there must be something wrong with me
There really must be
Something wrong
Deep down

Because I keep hearing about how these
Violent shows
Violent toys
And violent video games
Are the training ground
The breeding ground
For violent individuals
To go on violent killing sprees
but despite doing all of these things

All these violence confessions before you
All of this training I've spent hours and hours on
Over years
I must be un-trainable
Defective in some way
Because despite what these professionals say
After all that I did when I was younger
I have yet
To ever actually kill
A single
Person.

The Yearbook

I look through them sometimes
The high school yearbooks
I have them all,
From 2001 to 2004
Amazed at how different I look
In each photo
And how different my classmates look
Late night insomnia
Scanning facebook
I marvel at how similar
And different
Those same classmates look now
Some skinnier
Some fatter
Some balder
Some with more hair than ever
A couple of grey hairs
A couple of wrinkles
Some haven't aged a day
Some, no longer with us
But at the 10 year reunion
Seeing them up close again

James P. Wagner (Ishwa)

Realizing that we've all changed
And yet we are all the same kids
That were in those yearbook photos.

The Wake

Barely 6 months
After our 10 year high school reunion
I heard you were in a coma
A terrible car crash in Florida
You maneuvered in time to save
Your girlfriend,
Positioned the car so that your side
Of the vehicle would be hit

Broken ribs
Damaged leg
Head injury
Brain activity questionable
There was a GoFundMe fundraiser
For your medical bills
After making my donation
I shared the link with the facebook group
For our class
And was proud to see
Many names I recognized
Pop up with generous amounts
To contribute to the cause

A week later you were dead
We got word that they were bringing
Your body back to Northport
Your home town
So your friends and family
Could pay their respects.

At your wake they had pictures
Celebrating how many interesting things
You did during your 28 years
The place was filled with your family
And college friends
Talking about the impact your life
And death had had
On them all

You and me fought like cats and dogs in
high school
I would never have called you a friend back then
But that didn't matter now
You were class of 2004
And seeing you gone was hard

But almost as hard was looking around the wake
And seeing that despite the dozens of woeful

facebook replies
To the news
And the dozen or so financial contributions to
your medical bills
That only myself
And 2 other people
From the 300 plus members of our class
Who still lived locally
Had bothered
To show up.

A Look Back

I've always been on a first name basis
With insomnia
But lately we've been seeing more and more
Of each other.
Our minds go to strange places
When we are up late at night.

Having lived in the same town
My entire life
I've never been very far from the schools I went to
Growing up

Being restless enough to go on a late night walk
At 2 in the morning
Bouncing a handball in my hand
I found myself making my way towards
The high school
The same one I graduated from
More than ten years ago
The same one my father went to
And my mother went to
My late night walk lead me

Ten Year Reunion

Looking for a fountain of youth
I found myself seeing familiar sights
The old handball courts I spent lots of time on
With my friends
The entrance I went through every day to the small
commons
Where we started our mornings,
The football field
The gym entrance
As I kept walking I turned left, down the
other street
That gave me a good view of the main entrance
The 911 memorial fountain
The trees and plants, many still the same
That occupied the place
When I went there.
I could see the ghosts of those I grew up with
Sitting on the lawn,
Having lunch on the grass
Kicking balls around in the fields
Groups of people that might very well
Never assemble again
Everyone together for a finite period
Until life splits them up
And we go in so, so many different directions.
We had no idea how unique,

How one of a kind each of our experiences
would be
In these years when we figured ourselves out
Before our jobs or careers
Bills or families to support
Before life's pressures would grind at us
Day, after day, after day
When learning things, and doing things was our job
learning new skills
Developing ourselves
Into who we were going to be
For the rest of our lives
Whether we knew it or not.

Although the road ahead looks long
Looking back I see the road behind
Is longer than I remember it to be
And while I'm excited for what lies ahead
There is an occasional glance to the past
To time frozen like a picture
And the knowledge
That what lies there
Stays there forever.

About the Author

James P. Wagner (Ishwa) first walked into a Long Island poetry reading at age 17 and hasn't looked back since. At Dowling College he earned his BA and his MALS and has frequently been back to guest lecture. While there, he was heavily involved in their Spoken Word poetry club, founded "The Conspiracy," the college's genre fiction journal, and helped form the GSA (Gay-Straight Alliance.)

Also while at Dowling, James founded (by accident) Local Gems Press which has since become the unofficial publisher of Long Island poetry—handling yearly publications such as *Bards Annual, The Nassau County Poet Laureate Society Review, The Suffolk County Poetry Review, Freshet* for Fresh Meadow Poets (Queens) and recently published the *Long Island Quarterly 25th Anniversary* edition. Local Gems has also published over 50 titles by individual authors, over 20 anthologies, and has gained a national and international audience of poets and poetry fans.

He is one of the editors of the *Perspectives* series— poetry concerning autism and other disabilities which went on to become best-sellers. His own poetry including his flagship autism poem "His Disability" has appeared at the Naturally Autistic Conference in Vancouver and in *Naturally Autistic Magazine*. His essays and works on autism and autistic culture having appeared in *Naturally Autistic Magazine* which is distributed all over western Canada. He spent 2 years as a radio host for Naturally Autistic ANCA on the show "Human Potential."

James's science fiction and fantasy stories have appeared in more than 30 fiction publications and journals including *Mobius, Golden Visions, MBrane Science Fiction, Paradigm Shift* amongst others. He is also an essayist, and has had essays published in various publications on topics such as autism, martial arts, history and sociology.

He has had a very long but very unorthodox relationship with the martial arts and is currently a Tai Chi/Bagua practitioner. His online historical series about Benjamin Franklin has been used in high school classrooms and he is currently working on a book titled "Business Lessons from Benjamin Franklin."

His performance poetry takes some help from his time in musical theater. James has appeared in such plays as *Fiddler on the Roof, How To Succeed in Business Without Really Trying, Kiss me Kate, The Fantastiks, You're a Good Man Charlie Brown, Little Shop of Horrors* and others.

James is a proud graduate of Northport High School, and has lived in the Northport area his entire life. When not writing he enjoys laser tag, poker, cooking, documentaries, drumming, playing piano, drawing, painting, goofing around with Legos and performing.

Local Gems Poetry Press is a small Long Island based poetry press dedicated to spreading poetry through performance and the written word. Local Gems believes that poetry is the voice of the people, and as the sister organization of the Bards Initiative, believes that poetry can be used to make a difference.

Local Gems is the sister-organization of the Bards Initiative.

www.localgemspoetrypress.com

58017369R00048

Made in the USA
Charleston, SC
29 June 2016